The Superstar Curriculum

The Superstar Curriculum

■ ■ ■

A Teenager's Guide to Success in School and Life

Ryan Keliher BA, B.ED, MBA.

ISBN: 1537273981
ISBN 13: 9781537273983

I dedicate this book to those who believe that the brightest tomorrow begins today.

And to my family, who always make me feel like a superstar.

The stories in this book are all true, but names have been changed to respect the privacy of individuals.

Table of Contents

About the Book

My hope is that this book can help you find ways to use your school experience to achieve greater personal growth. School is about more than academics. As a teacher and coach for the past ten years, I've realized that even the highest of achievers are often unaware of certain skills, habits, or attitudes they lack—ones that could significantly improve their lives. *The Superstar Curriculum* explains how the greatest qualities and habits you can develop in school are not explicitly taught in class. The advice in this book will transform the way you approach school and set you up for a lifetime of achievement.

The good news is that you are already on your way to a life of superstardom. Certain chapters will reinforce some world-class traits that you already have, while other chapters will highlight areas for growth. The goal is to get the full package.

The Superstar Curriculum is divided into the four stages of superstardom:

Stage 1: Form Your Foundation for Success—You must build your success from the ground up by developing a strong personal character.

Stage 2: Work Your Way to Results You Want—If you want the best results in life, you need the best work ethic.

Stage 3: Optimize Your Opportunities—Your ability to make the most of your daily opportunities determines your levels of personal growth.

Stage 4: Become the Leader of Your Life—The most successful leaders understand that positive change must come from within.

There are **optional** reflection and self-awareness opportunities at the end of each chapter. Reflection is a wonderful way to move forward by looking back. Answering the chapter questions can improve your self-awareness and help you tailor the chapter's advice to your life. Reflection prompts your thinking; your thinking ignites action; your actions create habits; and your habits deliver results. Self-awareness is key to this book and vital to your personal growth.

Although some of the chapters relate to each other, you can read this book any way you want—front to back, back to front, or starting in the middle. All chapters are short; I know how busy teenagers are these days. You could read one chapter per day (roughly ten minutes) and change your life in less than a month. I tried to write the book I wish I'd had growing up. Are you ready? It's time to transform from student to superstar.

Prologue—Be Smart

The price of greatness is responsibility.

—Winston Churchill

This book is filled with advice. Let's face it: success is rarely achieved without help from others. I've always received the best advice from my dad—I still do today. He's a superstar in my life. What I like most about my father's advice is that he never lectures me or drags out our discussions. Here is one of my favorite examples:

Growing up I always wondered if I would get "the talk"—you know, the dreadful one-sided conversation parents have with their teenagers that makes those involved feel as if they should forever avoid eye contact. Well, it was my senior year of high school, and I had my first serious girlfriend. One blustery winter night, my father was driving me to her house (he didn't trust my winter driving), and as I was unbuckling my seatbelt about to leave the car, he lowered the volume on the radio, turned to me, and said, "Ryan, be smart."

That was it. That was "the talk." It lasted all of three words, but it was all I needed. His advice was so practical, so to the point, and so sensible that it tattooed itself on my brain. I knew what he was talking about—and he knew that I knew what he was talking about. And I know that you know what he was talking about.

Long before my father gave me those obvious words of advice, I was well aware that I should make smart decisions, but hearing him tell me to "be smart" made me feel responsible for my own actions. His words encouraged me to take control of my life and reaffirmed that I was in charge of my decisions and my life's direction. I welcomed a life of responsibility and accountability.

That is my hope for you. All the advice in this book is practical and to the point. After reading it, I hope that you will feel more responsible for your actions and take control of your life. I hope that you will want to "be smart." We are all capable of making good decisions, but there's a difference between knowing what's best and doing what's best. Leaders accept the responsibility to do what's best. You can become the greatest leader of your own life. When you do, you will inspire others to greatness too. That makes you a superstar.

Introduction—The Superstar Mind-Set

To live is the rarest thing in the world. Most people just exist, that is all.

—Oscar Wilde

True superstars live everywhere. Forget fortune and fame—the world's most legendary people, no matter their craft and notoriety, share a common attribute that drives achievement.

I call it the Superstar Mind-Set: a relentless desire to develop over time. Whether you speak of Mother Teresa or Michael Jordan, family members or friends, musicians or mechanics, those who are dedicated to personal development will achieve results, gain respect, and become sources of inspiration to others. So cool. So admirable. And best of all, so possible. With a superstar mind-set, you can become a superstar in all aspects of your life.

Developing a superstar mind-set requires focus and time, and as a teenager, you have the opportunity to focus much of your time in a place created for development. School offers a multitude of benefits, beyond the actual schoolwork, that can set you up for monumental success and unlimited personal growth. Every school is filled with superstar potential, but it isn't filled with superstars. Too many teenagers see school as an obligation instead of an opportunity. While some students believe school is a place to prepare them for the real world, those with a superstar mind-set understand that school is the real world. You can use your time in school to develop world-class qualities that will create superstar moments in your life. The more of these moments you create, the better your life will become.

Come graduation night when you walk across the stage to accept your diploma, people will be thinking, "That person is going to *wow* people wherever he or she goes in life." Superstars are in the business of *wowing* people. And once superstar status is achieved, other windows of opportunity begin flying open. Success takes time, and your time starts now.

Stage I

Form Your Foundation for Success

Intelligence plus character—that is the goal of true education.

—*Martin Luther King Jr.*

In order to reach your superstar potential, you must build a strong foundation. This stage focuses on using your time in school to develop principled habits that will strengthen your personal character.

1

Value First Impressions

A good first impression can work wonders.

—*J. K. Rowling*

You only ever get one chance at a first impression. At the beginning of every semester, I meet roughly one hundred new students. The first day is always a bit of a blur, but here is the usual situation: I remember a handful of students who make positive first impressions; I remember a few students who make negative first impressions; and I forget the rest who make no real impression on me (I eventually learn their names, I promise). People can form opinions about you—good or bad, true or not true—within the first few moments of meeting you. These first impressions are often lasting, so do yourself a favor and let the best version of you shine when meeting someone for the first time. Valuing first encounters is an easy way to stand out for all the right reasons.

Making an effective first impression can be simple. A few years ago, a student approached me after the first day of class and, with a smile on his face, he said, "It was nice meeting you today. See you tomorrow." He likely would not remember our little encounter, but it was genuine, kind, and so rare that it made a lasting impression on me. Never underestimate how big an impact even the smallest positive action can have on others. His actions weren't fake. He wasn't over the top. What he said was nice, and I appreciated the kind words. For the rest of the year, I thought highly of this student, and, looking back, there's no doubt that our simple yet memorable first encounter was a big reason why.

School provides you with opportunities to make positive first impressions on teachers, crushes, classmates—the list goes on. Here are some easy ways to help you make a positive first impression in school:

- *Be punctual.* (Or, if you're late, give your teacher an explanation. They love when you talk to them.)
- *Be prepared.* (Would you go to hockey without caring that you forgot your skates? It should be the same in class with a pencil.)
- *Know and respect rules.* (E.g., if you are not supposed to wear a hat, don't wear a hat. If you don't agree with a certain rule, have a conversation with someone in charge instead of simply defying the rule.)
- *Don't sit in the back.* (You don't have to be front and center, but avoid the back if you can. Perception is reality—I'll explain this in more detail in a later chapter.)
- *Greet people properly.* (Make eye contact and introduce yourself.)
- *Smile.* (It makes people feel happy and at ease. It also requires fewer muscles than frowning.)

- *Be yourself.* (Let your own personality shine. First impressions should be genuine.)

These simple tips give off friendly, warm vibes. People like warm vibes (that's why hot yoga is so popular).

Later in life you will meet people for the first time in various important moments. You'll meet your future girlfriend or boyfriend, husband or wife, bosses and friends. Using school to develop the habit of making positive first impressions will make these always-important-but-often-stressful situations easier.

A positive first impression garners mutual respect. Showing respect to others by giving them your best "you" will also result in your gaining their respect. Whether it is a classmate or a cashier, the next time you meet somebody, be the type of person you'd like to meet. If you forget the tips listed above, just be genuinely kind. The best kind of person is a kind person. Positive first impressions lead to positive relationships, so approach each new encounter like a star and shine bright. You will develop relationships that are out of this world.

Reflection and Self-Awareness Opportunity

1) *How effective are you at making positive first impressions?*

1	2	3	4	5
not good		fair		very good

2) *Create a list of people you could try to make a positive impression on in your life.*

   1.
   2.
   3.

3) *How could you go about creating these positive first impressions?*

   1.
   2.
   3.

2

Be a Class Act

Kind words are short and easy to speak, but their echoes are truly endless.

—*Mother Teresa*

We've all been told the importance of minding our manners, and being polite sounds easy in theory, but developing any superstar habit takes conscious effort and practice. In eleventh grade I had a teacher who used to tell my class that manners could get us just as far in life as good grades. I figured it was her way of getting the class to behave, but over time I have come to understand and appreciate her advice. When you are polite, people like you. People are more willing to help you. It really is that simple. Good manners can open doors for you that other skills and characteristics cannot.

Your words help create and reveal your character, so choose your vocabulary carefully. Make a habit of using terms associated with respect. Simple words, such as hello, good-bye, please, and thank you, are always appreciated no matter if you are speaking to a best friend or a bus driver. School is a tremendous environment in which to make good manners part of your identity because of the many social interactions that occur there every day. In the halls or at your locker, you will see people, bump into people, and cut people off accidentally. Be polite in those situations. Say hi, excuse me, or sorry! Greeting others and responding well to greetings brings positive energy into the world. Your manners can become an extension of you.

Being polite is also an easy, low-risk way to socialize in a positive fashion. Manners can provide naturally quiet people opportunities to speak in social situations and can serve as a springboard to launch further conversation. If you are genuinely polite, people are more likely to form a favorable opinion of you. As already discussed, first impressions are so important, and good manners only help in this regard. Manners can make you more social and memorable.

Although the words you use are important, your actions often speak even louder. Polite people help others, listen when someone speaks, and are mindful in social situations. For instance, being polite is difficult when your headphones are pumping music. There's a time and place for everything. And yes, sometimes having your headphones in is the polite thing to do (you almost got me there). The same goes for using your smartphone in social situations. Always think about how your actions might affect others, and act the way you want to be seen. Be someone who holds the door open for friends and strangers. Be a role model around children. Let your actions create positive reactions.

Developing good manners in school will help generate benefits in other aspects of your life. Manners can help you get a job or get a date and help you in your job and on your date. You can impress your boyfriend's or girlfriend's parents, get better service at a restaurant or hotel, and the list goes on. Using proper manners in everyday situations shows others that you are living in the moment. People appreciate that—in a world so full of distraction, it's becoming increasingly rare each day.

Tomorrow, track the words you use and the actions you display toward others. World-class companies are extremely mindful of the words they choose, and they pride themselves in their customer service. You can do the same. Choose respectful words and positive actions that strengthen your personal brand and lift others up. Allow your manners to make you a class act. Although our society seems so focused on aesthetics, always be more concerned about how you act than how you look. Twenty years from now, the clothes you are wearing today will no longer be popular, but the good manners you demonstrate will always be in style. Everyone loves a classic.

Reflection and Self-Awareness Opportunity

1) *When it comes to your manners, circle the statement that best applies to you:*
   a) *I am often not a polite person.*
   b) *I am a polite person, but my manners could use some work.*
   c) *I am a polite person but am more quiet than anything.*
   d) *I am a polite person.*

2) *List times when you could practice or improve upon your manners during the run of a school day:*
   a)
   b)
   c)

3) *Think about the types of words you use on a daily basis. How do they reflect your personal brand?*

4) *Try tracking your words and actions for a day. After doing so, what did you notice?*

3

Understand the Power of Perception

Some people feel the rain while others just get wet.

—Bob Marley

I once coached a player who always found herself in foul trouble during basketball games. After a referee would signal a foul, she'd often turn to me exclaiming, "But coach, I didn't foul her." Once the whistle blew, however, whether she had truly fouled her opponent no longer mattered because the situation was about perception. The reality for the referee was that a foul had been committed, yet the reality for her was that no foul had occurred. Could they both have been right? Not really, but sort of. You see, people's perceptions of things often shape their versions of reality. The sooner you understand this, the better your reality will become.

Reality differs for everybody. For instance, you may view yourself or your peer group in one light, while others might share a completely different opinion. This happens all the time. Sometimes versions of reality match up, and sometimes they don't. For this reason it is important to understand that others can (and will) perceive your behavior, attitude, and actions in ways that shape their reality.

Always consider how you are representing yourself in a given moment. If you appear lazy, someone will perceive you as lazy. If you appear kind, someone will view you as kind. If you appear rude, defiant, irresponsible (you get the point), others will perceive you as such. I'm not suggesting that you should always seek others' approval or live your life worrying about what others think of you—that's not healthy—but you should be mindful of your reputation. Good or bad, rightly or wrongly, it will follow you. Your reputation is often created as a result of your actions, which form people's perceptions and realities. Understanding this can help you make better decisions. Live your life the way you'd like to be perceived. Use school as a social and academic platform to build a reputation based on the admirable actions you display. Doing so will improve your reality.

■ ■ ■

Just as it's important to understand that others will create their versions of reality based on perception, it's also important to understand how perception can frame your own reality. Henry Ford, founder of Ford Motor Company and superstar innovator, put it best when he said, "Whether you think you can, or you think you can't—you're right." If you believe that you cannot achieve something, the reality is that you likely will not achieve it. If you view your life as negative, then negative energy will fuel your days. But if you believe that something is achievable, it will more likely become a reality. Perceiving every day as an opportunity allows positivity to rule your day. Your thoughts drive your actions. Changing your outlook on life can change your life.

Positive people live more positive days. When you learn to focus on your possibilities instead of your problems, anything becomes achievable. Superstar tennis champion Roger Federer had the right idea when he said, "I think I am great; therefore, I am." Allow your perception to lift you instead of limit you. Too often we build our own imaginary walls that confine our lives. Far too many students limit themselves personally, academically, and socially because of their life circumstances, past experiences, or personal doubts. Break down these walls and find the courage to explore an existence where anything is possible. Think like Federer, and understand that you are capable of amazing feats. Never let your perception overpower your potential. When you look in the mirror, see the superstar that exists within you. Believing always precedes achieving.

To sum up, imagine a world where everyone wears glasses and each individual prescription is a person's perception of things. Always be aware of how you might look through someone else's lenses. And when it comes to your own prescription, make sure you are getting regular checkups. If your own lenses start limiting your vision, get a new prescription that enables you to see all the wondrous possibilities that exist in front of you. Perception will help create your future reality. If you try to become a person you'd love, then you'll love the person you'll become. And everyone else will love you too.

Reflection and Self-Awareness Opportunity

1) *What is your current perception of life?*
   a) *Negative*
   b) *Somewhat negative*
   c) *Haven't really thought about it*
   d) *Somewhat positive*
   e) *Positive*

If you answered A, B, or C, try writing down three positive aspects of your life. Remember, changing your outlook on life can change our life.

2) *How do you think your teachers generally perceive your actions, attitudes, and behaviors in school?*
   a) *Negatively*
   b) *Somewhat negatively*
   c) *Hard to say*
   d) *Somewhat positively*
   e) *Positively*

If you answered A, B, or C, write down some changes you could make in your life to improve others' perceptions of you.

3) *What are some imaginary walls that you've built for yourself? What are some potential benefits of breaking down these walls?*

4

Know That You Are Part of Something Bigger

It is our collective and individual responsibility to preserve and tend to the environment in which we all live.

—DALAI LAMA

It's astounding how many various networks exist in our lives. In all of these different circles, we are the common denominators, so it's often easy to think of our own interests first. It's important to realize, however, that we are always part of something much bigger than ourselves. This understanding brings an attitude of collective responsibility. By understanding and embracing our individual responsibility to positively affect others, we often make better life decisions and, in doing so, make the world a better place. That's a rewarding way to live.

In your life today, some of your various networks could include:

- Your family
- Your friend groups
- Your school
- Your work

- Your sports team
- Your band
- Your other clubs/groups
- Your province/state/country
- Your world

Your actions (and the actions of others) affect these networks. School, which is a community of its own, allows you to practice being part of something bigger because it's a place where small actions can impact a large group. For example, if all students left their waste at the cafeteria table after eating lunch, what kind of mess would it create? Now extend this cafeteria example to our precious planet. Scary, I know, but that is how collective responsibility works. Thinking of personal convenience instead of collective responsibility often results in shortsighted judgments, bad decisions, and future consequences for yourself and others. It is only when we think of how our actions best serve others that we end up best serving ourselves.

Your environment is more than physical; it's also social. Communication and collaboration skills are some of the most highly regarded skills for twenty-first-century workers (that's you), so capitalize on these developmental opportunities in school. Unfortunately, when working in a group, many students fail to do their fair share, knowing that others will eventually pick up their slack. Don't be one of those people. If you make selfish decisions (ones where you think solely of your own benefit), then the collective whole, of which you are a part, suffers. Whether you are working as a group in a class, as part of a team, or a member of your family, know that your attitude, work ethic, and actions will affect others. Group experiences, where everyone produces at their highest levels, will produce some of your most memorable moments and rewarding results.

Legendary football coach Vince Lombardi said, "Individual commitment to a group effort—that is what makes a team work, a company work, a society work, and a civilization work." Contributing to your various groups in meaningful ways by putting forth your finest effort is a perfect way to lead by example. The world needs more of these everyday leaders working together; that's how the biggest problems are solved. Mindful people, committed to a greater cause, refine the world.

If you envision a world where everyone understands that they are part of something bigger, the world quickly becomes a beautiful place with so much potential for growth. Imagine if everyone went out of their way to help others; if everyone made more personal sacrifices for the greater good; if everyone wore seatbelts, quit smoking, and decided to never drink and drive. Imagine if everyone stopped being hurtful because they understood how their words and actions negatively affect others. If you, just you, understand the collective power of these individual actions, the world will thank you. You'll drive positive change, inspire others, and make the world a better place—that's superstar material.

PS: Read or listen to the news to inform yourself of the bigger picture. It's unfortunate that mostly bad news is broadcast, but hearing it can put life in perspective and help you realize that your problems might be more manageable than you originally thought. Plus, how can you help solve the world's problems if you don't know they exist? The world needs you to care about it. We are all in this together. All right. Hands in. Team on three.

Reflection and Self-Awareness Opportunity

1) *Think of a group/network in which you are currently involved. Now think about your actions within the group. How have your actions affected the group?*

Group/Network:

Actions:

Affect:

2) *What is an issue in your community, country, or world that is important to you? Do some online reading to learn more about it. See if you can help!*

5

Get to Know the Friends Who Aren't Your Friends

Surround yourself with only people who are going to take you higher.

—OPRAH WINFREY

Socializing is a huge element of your total school experience. If you have a social circle where you feel happy, that's awesome. If you don't have a friend group that makes you happy, then what you have is an opportunity. And opportunities are awesome, too.

Depending on the size of your school, you could have hundreds or even thousands of potential friends in your building. You won't become friends with everybody. In fact, you may even dislike some people, and not everyone will like you either. Don't stress it. We are not all compatible. That being said, just because you can't be friends with everyone doesn't mean you can't be friendly with everyone. Interacting in a friendly fashion is a sure way to improve your social circle, your life, and the lives of others. Triple win.

The best way to make a friend is to be one. Remember that best friend you met on the first day of kindergarten? How do you think that relationship started? Chances are it was from being friendly without judgment. The concept still works today, but, unfortunately, many students go years without speaking to or smiling at one another. Not because they dislike one another but because they don't know one another. When you think about this situation, it is circular in logic. Students won't speak to certain people because they don't know them, yet the reason they don't know them is because they won't speak to them. This leads to students forming opinions of people before actually knowing them. Judging people before getting to know them likely says more about your character than it does about those you judge.

Take a chance on friendship. In order for two people to meet, someone must initiate communication. Let that someone be you. Although this might take courage, the results can be incredible. Ben Cohen and Jerry Greenfield, co-founders of the successful ice cream company Ben & Jerry's, first met by striking up a conversation in a seventh grade gym class (and the rest is delicious, delicious history!). The person sitting beside you could become your best friend, significant other, or business partner you go on to make millions with, but only if you are willing to be a friend first. It's an opportunity worth exploring.

You improve any environment when you recognize the existence, and celebrate the differences, of others. Imagine if everyone in your school was friendly to people who weren't their "friends." These actions can take the form of greetings, smiles, small talk, or offers to help. You have the power to make the world a friendlier place—a better place. When it comes to friendship, the only thing better than having a friend who brings out the best in you is being that friend to others. There's always someone who needs a friend. Help lead the world to happiness.

Friends Who Aren't Your Friends—Part II

It's important to look closely at your social circle to determine whether the friends you have are truly your friends. Sadly, upon reflection (real, honest reflection), some people realize that certain friends are actually not true friends at all.

It is sad seeing students whose social circles bring them down. Friends who are envious of you in a negative way, put you down, pressure you to do things you don't want to do, or pressure you to not do things you do want to do are not true friends. If such people make up your social circle, speak with them and reestablish what friendship means. If they are true friends, things will improve. If they don't respect what you have to say, the truth is you may be better off without that relationship in your life. Leaving a social group and attempting to make new friends is easier said than done, but sometimes the smartest decisions are the toughest decisions. Your time and your life are too valuable for toxic relationships.

You become a combination of the people you spend most of your time with, so choose only the finest of friends. Real friends are proud of you. They lift you up, respect you, and encourage you to be yourself and follow your dreams. And as a friend, you should be doing the same to yours. Boxing superstar Muhammad Ali said, "Friendship… is not something you learn in school. But if you haven't learned the meaning of friendship, you really haven't learned anything." School is a place where friendships develop, so use the opportunity to learn about one of life's most precious gifts. If you surround yourself with true friends, one day you'll look back on your life with countless memories of time shared with people you love. That sounds pretty good to me.

Reflection and Self-Awareness Opportunity

1) *How comfortable do you feel talking to people who aren't your "friends?"*

    A) *Not comfortable at all*
    B) *Somewhat comfortable*
    C) *Comfortable*
    D) *Very comfortable*

Write down an opportunity when you could reach out to someone who is not your "friend".

2) *Think about your core group of friends. Are you happy with whom you are surrounding yourself? Why or why not?*

3) *Think about the way your treat your core group of friends. Are you acting the way a true friend should? Why or why not?*

6

Be Good to Everyone

No matter what happens in life, be good to peo-ple. Being good to people is a wonderful legacy to leave behind.

—Taylor Swift

The way you treat others often determines the way people remember you. My school's principal emphasizes that the character of our school is defined by the way we care for our most vulnerable students. This mantra resonated with me strongly as a teacher, and it has greatly improved my mindfulness of how I treat others on a daily basis. The reality is that kind people aren't always kind and mean people aren't always mean, but everyone is something in any given moment. If you become mindful of the way you treat others in each moment, kindness will prevail and people will prosper.

Unfortunately, school isn't always a kind place. Bullies can make life a living nightmare for others. In some cases, bullies don't understand the destruction of their words or actions. My heart aches for all victims of bullying, but it's hard to fault someone who truly doesn't know the difference between what's right and what's wrong. Other instances in which bullies are aware of their hurtful actions are shameful. These incidents, which occur at alarming rates, are character crushers for both the bully and the victim. That's why education is so important. It brings enlightenment, acceptance, and maturity.

Nobody is perfect. We all have insecurities, we all have weaknesses, and we've all made mistakes—we don't need others to magnify them for us. I could give an example of a specific situation of bullying (sadly, I could give a hundred examples), but highlighting one situation would make it seem like it was worse than the rest. Whether you poke fun in person or behind someone's back, online or offline, in seriousness or in jest, preying on someone's weaknesses (mental, physical, or emotional) is never funny or cool. Kindness is cool. One act of kindness can be all it takes to make others feel better about their lives. It doesn't get much cooler than that.

Opportunities to be unkind to others will occur at school, and the way you act will reveal your character.

- If people are making fun of another student, will you join in? Or will you stand up for that person?
- If the person in the cafeteria line is shy, will you jump in line in front of him? Or will you patiently wait your turn even though you know you could save yourself some time at his expense?
- If someone embarrasses herself, will your actions make her feel worse? Or will you attempt to make her feel better?

Use these opportunities to demonstrate integrity and lift others up. Similar scenarios will continue to occur in different environments for the rest of your life. Some people will always try to get ahead by taking advantage of others and bringing them down. This shallow approach might even appear to work at first, but its effectiveness will be short lived. Kindness will always outlast hatred. Integrity runs deep from the heart, so if you live a life of integrity, you will never be a shallow person.

You cannot control the actions of others, but you can always control how you act toward others. Let your actions better the lives of those around you. When you view everyone as equal, you live a life that is centered on respect. But remember, in order to respect everyone, you must start with yourself. Expect the best of yourself. Have the highest standards. Strive for greatness. Instill integrity into your life. When you act in a way that earns people's respect, you create a culture of civility that endures throughout your life.

It's often said that respect must be earned, meaning that you must prove yourself to others in order to gain their respect. This is true. But respect is also learned. If you learn to treat others with respect to begin with, then you'll find yourself in respectful situations more often. Being good to everyone is a superstar quality that elevates your life and the lives of those around you. When your head hits the pillow each night, you will fall asleep a little easier knowing you are a person who appreciates every life. And who doesn't love a good night's sleep?

Reflection and Self-Awareness Opportunity

1) *Write down a time when you (or others) took advantage of someone:*

2) *Looking back, what could you learn from this experience? What could it teach you about respect? What could have been done differently?*

7

Be a Goal Setter

As soon as I accomplish one thing, I just set a higher goal. That's how I've gotten to where I am.

—*Beyoncé*

In sports, scoring goals can make you a superstar. In life, setting goals can do the same. Successful people and goals go together like birthdays and cakes. Every year I meet students with big dreams, which is the way it should be, but it always amazes me how few students have set goals to help them achieve their dreams. Too many students just hope that someday everything will work out for them. In life, greatness requires goals.

Setting goals aligns your realities of today with your dreams of tomorrow, but being smart is key when planning your steps to success. Peter Drucker popularized a simple, **SMART** framework, which makes creating and achieving goals more manageable. SMART is an acronym that stands for **S**pecific, **M**easurable, **A**ttainable, **R**ealistic, and **T**ime-bound. Formulating goals using this framework allows you to start small while dreaming and achieving big.

Being SMART about your goals is being smart about your life. For instance, the goal to **"get in shape"** is well intended but is too vague, which makes it more of a hope than a goal. Using the SMART framework, you can better write this goal as **"Exercise for one hour, four days per week, for two months."** This changes a vague hope to get in shape into an achievable SMART goal with defined characteristics:

- This goal is *Specific* because it lays out what exactly is to be achieved.
- It's *Measurable* because you can track whether you make it to the gym for one hour, four days per week.
- It's *Attainable* and *Realistic* because it's not suggesting you must work out all day every day—only one hour per day, four days per week.
- And it's *Time-bound* because the two-month time frame keeps you motivated and accountable to stick to your plan.

Once a SMART goal is set, the next step is to consider what actions will help you achieve your goal. In this example, beneficial actions could be to create a workout plan, eat healthy, and get enough rest. Every goal needs an action plan. If you want to be an engineer, or own a car, or travel the world, think about the steps you could take to help you achieve your desires. Will you need a good education? Money management skills? People skills? Remember, your actions create your habits. When your actions become goal-driven, achieving your goals will become a habit.

Although the future is unknown, you can still create a clear vision for yourself by setting SMART goals that serve as your foundation for living. Just because you don't know what colors you're going to paint the walls of a new house doesn't mean you can't start laying the foundation. SMART goals provide you with a solid structure on which to build your future. They sharpen your focus and help you become the person you dream of being. With properly set goals, life will happen for you instead of happening to you. You'll go where you want to go, and you'll be happier because you brought yourself there. So much of school is performance based that it allows you multiple opportunities to set goals. These can relate to academics, sports, theater, personal growth, or any other curricular or extracurricular activity. If you start setting short-term goals now, you'll live an ambitious life filled with purposeful actions. That is one stellar combo.

Superstars are more than dreamers; they are doers. Walt Disney, a creative superstar who was once fired from a newspaper outlet for lacking creativity, believed that "all of our dreams can come true, if we have the courage to pursue them." Chase your dreams, and set SMART goals to make the chase easier. Write your goals down, and pin them up. Tell your friends about them, and establish a support network to help you along the way. Hold yourself accountable, and set expectations that promote development. Start small. Work hard. Achieve big. Then repeat. That's the evolution of a true superstar. Keep changing your world for the better.

Note: Although this is the end of this chapter, there are three important elements to also consider when achieving your goals. The importance of persistence—you'll often have to fight through the darkness of defeat before experiencing the bright lights of success. The importance of sacrifice—your biggest dreams will require great sacrifice. And the importance of happiness—you can't be so focused on future goals that you lose sight of your present happiness. These traits are so important that they deserve chapters of their own.

Reflection and Self-Awareness Opportunity

Remember, be SMART when goal setting. (Specific, Measurable, Attainable, Realistic, Time-bound).
*"**I will do better in school**" is better written:*
***"I will increase my grades 10% by the end of the school year.**"*
Action plan:

- *Ask more questions in class when I'm unsure of course concepts.*
- *Study for tests without the distraction of my phone.*
- *Practice the effective listening strategies from Chapter 19 of this book.*

1) ***Dream BIG:*** *Write down one long-term goal (beyond one year from now).*

Action plan: What could you do in the short-term to help achieve your long-term goal?

2) ***Start small:*** *Write down one short-term goal (within the year).*

Action plan: What tasks could you perform to help you achieve your goal?

Stage II

Work Your Way to Results You Want

The three great essentials to achieve anything worthwhile are: Hard work, Stick-to-itiveness, and Common sense.

—*Thomas Edison*

If you want to create the best life, you need the best work ethic. This stage focuses on developing superstar qualities centered on hard work, which will help you achieve remarkable results in school and life.

8

Hone Your Work Ethic

What separates the talented individual from the successful one is a lot of hard work.

—STEPHEN KING

The students in my tenth-grade literature class are always shocked when I tell them that I do not care about their grades. It sounds odd, but it is true. I earned three university degrees and have had various jobs and multiple interviews, and nobody ever asked about my tenth-grade literature mark (even when I was hired to teach the course!). It mattered that I had passing grades in order to move along in the education system, but whether I earned 60 percent or 90 percent, A+ or C-, did not matter. What mattered were my skills, which were honed as a result of my work ethic. The truth is that the work ethic you develop in school is far more important than any grade you will ever receive.

In order for your grade to have true meaning, you should follow this equation:

WORK ETHIC + ABILITY = YOUR GRADE

It is what's behind your grade that matters. When looking at the variables of this equation, you cannot necessarily control your cognitive abilities, but you can always control your work ethic.

Let me use two former students (of whom there are hundreds more just like them) as examples of why you should focus on work ethic over grades:

Jenna found schoolwork not easy, but not hard either. She attended class, did her work, and put forth a decent effort that resulted in a respectable grade of 80 percent. She knew deep down that she coasted through school, but it was OK because her grades were high enough to keep everyone (her parents, her teachers, and herself) happy.

Erin, on the other hand, found schoolwork difficult. Not impossible, but challenging. She attended class, did her work, and put forth her best effort in order to receive a respectable grade of 80 percent. Her drive and determination resulted in her grades being high enough to keep everyone (her parents, her teachers, and herself) happy.

Jenna and Erin's identical grades of 80 percent suggest that they are on equal footing as students. This might be true for a school transcript, but it's not true in life. There is no score keeping in the game of life, so instead of concentrating on your grades, focus on playing the game the right way. It's understandable that parents and teachers might be happy when your grades meet their satisfaction levels, but that doesn't mean you should necessarily be happy too. Only you truly know how hard you work and how much you challenge yourself. You know when you can do more, and you also know when you do your best. Be honest with yourself. Have high expectations. And celebrate a job well done. Regardless of your intellectual ability, you can identify with Erin because you can always control your work ethic.

There is no doubt that being naturally bright in school is a helpful quality, but it can also prove hurtful if external grades are your primary focus. So many students coast through school earning satisfactory grades that keep their parents and teachers happy. All appears great, but these students know deep down that they are capable of better work. The problem with coasting is that they can only coast in one direction - downhill. While students coast, opportunities to develop internally driven qualities that fuel a person's rise to success, such as self-discipline, resilience, or persistence zoom by them. They might acquire these valuable traits someday, but they could have to learn a hard lesson first. It could cost them a job, a spot on the team, or a role in the play. I suggest that you skip the hard lesson by finding the self-motivation to improve your work ethic. Self-motivation, or lack thereof, transfers to other areas of your life. If you coast in one place, you'll coast in another place. If doing your best becomes a habit, you'll astonish yourself and others.

Giving your realest effort is a gratifying and rewarding way to live. The hard work you do won't always be fun, but if you strive for greatness, you'll thrive in life. Legendary artist Michelangelo said, "If people knew how hard I work to gain my mastery, it wouldn't seem wonderful at all." Become the Michelangelo of your class, your team, or your family. Master your work ethic, and build a life that is a masterpiece. Remember that superstar habits are developed over time. Humans are creatures and creators of habit, so be the hardest-working creature and create the greatest habits. Work your way to the results you want.

PS: It's important to note that grades are valuable in many circumstances, but just because you need certain grades to graduate, get into postsecondary school, or attain certain scholarships still doesn't mean you should focus on grades. If you focus on your work ethic, the grades will follow. And if you focus on the advice from Stage I of this book, getting glowing reference letters from teachers will be a breeze.

Reflection and Self-Awareness Opportunity

1) *Think back to your last year of school. Were you good at pushing yourself? Was your work ethic more like Jenna's (who coasted more often than worked hard) or more like Erin's (who worked hard more often than coasted)?*

If you picked Jenna, what could you do to improve?

If you picked Erin, write down things you did well so you remember to keep them up!

2) *Write about a time when you worked really hard to accomplish something. How did you feel afterward?*

9

Develop Resilience Daily

It is not the strongest of species that survive, nor the most intelligent, but the ones most resilient and responsive to change.

—Charles Darwin

We live in a wonderful world, but it's not without problems and challenges that are beyond our control. You will face hardships throughout your life that are unsolvable on your own—in those moments, be thankful for people who support and guide you. Some problems should not be tackled solo. But the truth is, in everyday life, what we sometimes consider a problem isn't much of a problem at all but simply an inconvenience. Knowing how to battle through life's daily inconveniences develops resilience—a superstar quality that exists in the world's most successful people.

Resilience is your ability to recover from setbacks. For a variety of reasons, life often does not go exactly as planned. Having the wherewithal to bounce back from unfortunate situations strengthens your character and improves your life. School brings many opportunities to find solutions to everyday obstacles, yet every year I see students who lack the resilience needed to solve daily challenges. For instance, when essays are due in my classes, there are often students who will say, "Mr. Keliher, I don't have my essay because my printer broke," and then look at me as if this situation is no longer their concern but mine. The way you choose to deal with an inconvenience like a broken printer says a lot about your mind-set and ability to overcome challenges.

Resilient people are problem solvers. You don't have to be an expert in printer repair to solve the issue of a broken printer. You could save your assignment to a jump drive. You don't have a jump drive? Borrow one from a friend. All your friends are asleep? Save your assignment online. Not tech savvy? Take pictures of your essay to show your teacher in the morning. No camera? Well, you might just have to go old school and write it out by hand (your grandparents would be proud). Always consider alternative solutions before giving up or offloading your inconveniences onto others. Although certain solutions may initially seem more annoying than resilient, champions see the value in doing the harder things in life. Writing an essay out by hand is not my idea of fun, but working through a setback (in this case to meet a deadline—an important life skill) is a character-building quality that will serve you well for the rest of your life.

Resilient people are fighters from whom we can learn so much. Terry Fox. Helen Keller. If you don't know their stories, I urge you to look them up—both amazingly resilient people who inspired millions. Or how about professional surfer Bethany Hamilton? If she can survive a shark attack that took her arm, yet return to surfing and become a champion, surely we can find ways to overcome life's minor setbacks. Imagine Bethany Hamilton as your teacher. Now imagine telling her that you gave up trying to find a way to print off your essay. Bethany Hamilton may not be your teacher by title, but she delivers a tremendous lesson on how your mind-set greatly determines your ability to tackle challenges.

Developing resilience begins with life's little problems. Use your time in school as an opportunity to overcome inconveniences. Put in the extra effort to get your work done well and on time. Find a tutor when learning gets tough. Ask questions when you need help. Don't allow obstacles to serve as excuses. A resilient mind-set, coupled with hard work and support networks, will enable you to face any challenge with optimism. Pushing through a set-back brings toughness, patience, and wisdom. This is important because you will rely on resilience for the rest of your life. As you grow up, you'll be faced with inconveniences, many of which will have higher stakes than a broken printer. Finding solutions to life's smaller challenges now better prepares you to conquer bigger set-backs that will inevitably come your way. Instead of folding when times get tough, you will flourish.

Note: Remember, not every problem is an inconvenience that can be solved on your own. You will encounter problems throughout your life when you'll need the help, guidance, and love of others. Life's toughest challenges are better solved together, so tapping into support networks during these times is the right thing to do. If you are ever dealing with mental illness, a low sense of self-worth, or any confusing time in your life, it's so important that you speak to someone. There will always be someone willing to help. Sometimes seeking support is the bravest, most resilient thing you can do.

Reflection and Self-Awareness Opportunity

1) *List a recent setback that occurred in your life:*

Circle the statement that best describes how you dealt with the situation:

a) *I was resilient. I recovered from my setback.*
b) *I lacked resilience. I offloaded my problem onto someone else.*
c) *I didn't do anything about my problem. I basically gave up.*
d) *I tried to solve the problem on my own, but I should have sought support.*

2) *List a challenge where you needed to seek outside support. What was the benefit of using a support network?*

10

Discover the Importance of Persistence

The greatest glory in living lies not in never falling, but in rising every time we fall.

—NELSON MANDELA

Persistence is a life-changing quality that allows you to battle through adversity and obstacles until you find success. It is similar to resilience in that they are both internally driven, but also complimentary, in that where resilience allows you to bounce back, persistence keeps you moving forward.

Success is most rewarding when it is a culmination of hard work that has paid off over a series of difficult times. In business, entrepreneurs who lack persistence typically don't last. They begin to doubt themselves, they lose motivation, and they eventually disappear. Legendary innovator Steve Jobs said that "about half of what separates the successful entrepreneurs from the non-successful ones is pure perseverance." What holds so many back is not a lack of intelligence or skill, but an unwillingness to persevere. For Steve Jobs, his rise to superstardom was filled with tumultuous times and unsuccessful moments, but his belief in himself and his vision for Apple products never wavered. Persistence is key to growth and success, not just in business, but also in school and in life.

We are often told to not be afraid of failure, but this is only sound advice if you have the persistence to progress through challenges. When you choose to battle through adversity, failure becomes nothing to fear because it is no longer an endpoint. Legendary basketball coach John Wooden said, "Failure is not fatal, but failure to change might be." Take responsibility and allow your failures to inform you. Let your challenges create positive change. With a persistent mind-set, failure is just another step along your ever-changing path toward success.

School is a perfect environment to begin bursting through life's roadblocks. Unfortunately, too many students choose to give up instead of rise up during tough times. Throughout school you will have courses, teachers, and projects that make your life difficult for a variety of reasons. Life might even seem unfair at certain points. But just because a course is complex, a teacher is tough, or a project is a pain, don't relinquish your effort. Learning to persist through turbulent times is one of the ultimate lessons you can ever learn in school. It will prove more beneficial than any single course or assignment ever will. Plus, if you persist you'll more than likely conquer whatever it is that is posing difficulty. It's a win-win.

Developing a mind-set of persistence now will help you deal with future tough times. There will be occasions, much more challenging than any course or assignment, when you will feel like giving up. Finding the drive to fight your own daily battles now will make moving forward much easier. Moments will occur throughout your lifetime when family, friends, and loved ones endure extreme hardships and want to crumble. You can provide an attitude of strength, optimism, and hope for others by never giving up. Persistence is a champion's mind-set and a life-changing habit. If you start developing it now, you'll rise to the occasion when you or others need it. Persistence brings achievement, inspiration, and admiration—all of which are superstar qualities.

Reflection and Self-Awareness Opportunity

1) *Overall, do you consider yourself a person who practices persistence?*
   Yes *No*

2) *Write down a few tough situations that have occurred in your life (in school or out of school) where showing persistence was needed.*
   Situation 1:
   Situation 2:
   Situation 3:

3) *Put a check mark beside the answer that best describes how effective you were at showing persistence in each situation.*

Situation 1:	*Situation 2:*	*Situation 3:*
A) Very good	*A) Very good*	*A) Very Good*
B) Good	*B) Good*	*B) Good*
C) So-so	*C) So-so*	*C) So-so*
D) Not good	*D) Not good*	*D) Not good*
E) Bad	*E) Bad*	*E) Bad*

4) *How did you feel after the situation was over? Why did you feel the way you did?*
   Situation 1:
   Situation 3:
   Situation 3:

11

Make Friends With Momentum

An object at rest stays at rest and an object in motion stays in motion…

—Sir Isaac Newton

Beginning something is the first step toward achieving anything. Picture trying to roll out of your cozy bed on a cold morning—hitting the snooze button and lying wrapped in warm blankets for an extra five minutes is always easy, and the idea of getting up and starting your day can seem impossible, but once you are out of bed for five minutes, being awake becomes easy too (most days). The reason the idea of getting moving seems daunting some mornings is because you have yet to build any momentum in your day. Once you understand the power of building positive momentum, getting up and getting results become easier. Momentum can make you unstoppable.

In order to build momentum, you have to start something. I mean really start something. For example, some people suggest that saving money for a new car is impossible without saving that first dollar.

This advice, although painfully obvious, is valuable because saving your first dollar gets you started, which is so important. However, with only one single dollar saved, you could go spend that dollar and not care much (it was only one dollar saved for a car that costs thousands). Having no positive momentum makes motivation and dedication more difficult.

Beginning something creates a beginner's mind-set, but manufacturing momentum creates a master's mind-set. If you save your first $100 instead of simply one dollar, then, all of a sudden, your mind-set changes. You begin to envision yourself behind the steering wheel of your new car. This is momentum building. It's important that you started with a first dollar, but with $100 saved, you are much more than started. You are on your way! Dedicating money to your car fund now becomes easier. That $100 quickly becomes $200, then $600, then $1600, and then, before you know it…Vroom! Vroom! Momentum can get you cruising in life.

Many students struggle in school because they never capitalize on the power of momentum. In the worst instances, students don't start anything, in which case there is little hope. In more common instances, however, students start something but their starts amount to very little. They have a beginner's mind-set. They pick up the pen. Read the first chapter. They do a little bit of work here, put in a little bit of effort there, and do a little bit of nothing over here. They go to school all week but stay home on Friday. They study for one test and wing it on another. This "momentumless" lifestyle is repeated in some instances for school years at a time! Many of these students have good intentions but never reap the benefits of momentum, thereby making achievement harder than it has to be.

Getting to a point where you benefit from momentum requires discipline and consistency. For instance, studying for one test is good, but having the discipline to study for a few tests in a row makes studying a habit. Studying then becomes easier, and you learn more. Mastering one chord on a guitar is gratifying, but mastering three chords through consistent practice can make you the life of a party. This makes you want to master more chords and more songs. Eating healthy and exercising for one day is smart, but keeping it up for two months will boost your energy and have you feeling awesome. Having the discipline to stay focused on your goals will create the consistent momentum needed to improve your productivity and results.

Use school to help you develop an unstoppable mind-set that builds positive momentum. Whether it is in your class, in your band, with your sports team, or with your friends, commit to building positive momentum into everything you do. Show up consistently. Work hard. Set SMART goals. Stay on track. And fight for results. Creating positive momentum for yourself now will put you in motion for a life of success. Instead of hitting the snooze button on life, your daily decisions will make your life a dream come true.

Note: Understand that momentum works both ways. It can accelerate your path to success or transport you to depths of despair. I've seen too many students gain such negative momentum that it transformed their lives in ways they would never have thought possible. Try to keep your momentum moving in a positive direction, but know that you will lose steam at times. Everyone does. When this happens, reflect, regroup, and refocus your priorities. Doing so will rebuild positive momentum. Generating momentum is easy when life is going well; it's when life is tough that positive momentum is harder to create, but the benefits of creating it are greater too. Resilience + Persistence = Positive Momentum.

Reflection and Self-Awareness Opportunity

1) *Write down a time in your life when you felt you built positive momentum:*

2) *How did you build that positive momentum?*

3) *Write down an area in your life where you have struggled to build momentum.*

4) *What could you do to create momentum in this area?*

12

Succeed through Sacrifice

The good and the great are only separated by their willingness to sacrifice.

—Kareem Abdul-Jabbar

You can do almost anything in this world, but you can't do everything. This is especially true if you want to do things well. The most ambitious achievements often require great sacrifice. Every year I speak to students who have goals they wish to achieve in school, music, sports, or other pursuits, which is exciting. But many of these students aren't prepared to make the sacrifices necessary to fully achieve their goals. Once you begin to understand the importance of sacrifice, you will begin to achieve more of your goals. Sometimes you must give up a little to gain a lot.

Growing up, I had a best friend named Corey. We were classmates every year, played on the same sports teams, and had the same friend group until eleventh grade when Corey moved from our small town in Atlantic Canada to join a junior hockey team halfway across the country. Corey had a dream (a.k.a. long-term goal) of playing with the stars in the National Hockey League (NHL). Joining this junior team was an important action in pursuit of his goal. In his rookie season with his new junior hockey team, Corey tallied only five points in fifty-seven games. That was hardly NHL material.

When his hockey season ended, I was excited for Corey to move back home so we could pick up where we had left off as best friends. He did move home and it was exciting, but we didn't pick up exactly where we had left off. We were still best friends, but Corey was often busy training or going to bed early so he would be energized for practice the next day. These sacrifices were not easy for Corey. He loved socializing with friends and was often the life of a party, but becoming a professional hockey player was going to take hours of training, and Corey was motivated and willing to make the necessary sacrifices. The most rewarding sacrifices are often the hardest ones to make.

To this day Corey and I remain friends, but because of his sacrifices, from that summer on, we didn't see each other as much. I did see Corey on national TV, however, a few years ago, blasting his first NHL goal past legendary goalie Martin Brodeur. Corey made it! He achieved his dream, and his sacrifices were a big reason why.

When trying to achieve a goal, sometimes what you don't do matters just as much as what you do. Because teenagers today are busier than ever before, it is important to know how to set your priorities in order to know what to sacrifice. Prioritizing means looking at your life's to-do list of wants and needs and determining the order in which the list should be completed. Putting your most important to-dos higher on your list makes sacrificing lower priorities easier. For example, if studying for your math test is high on your priority list, then an activity such as watching a movie, which would usually be more appealing than studying, becomes an easier sacrifice. In Corey's case, training to achieve his dream of playing in the NHL became his biggest priority, so he filled his life with actions that matched his priority. Ensuring that your priorities are in line with your goals will improve your decision making. Making sacrifices based on your top priorities won't always be easy because we often want to try to do it all, but sticking to your priorities will always be worth it. You will live a life that follows your preferred path.

Think about your goals in school and life and consider what sacrifices you could make to better achieve those goals. These sacrifices will differ in type and size. Whether it is forgoing junk food for healthier food choices, sacrificing new clothes for college savings, or passing up on a party for piano practice, learning to sacrifice will help you realize what is truly important in your life. Sacrifice often separates the person who wants something to happen from the person who makes something happen. If you learn to sacrifice today, you'll find yourself in a better place tomorrow. As my father used to tell me, short-term pain for long-term gain. Superstardom does not exist without sacrifice.

Reflection and Self-Awareness Opportunity

1) *What are three current priorities when it comes to creating your preferred future? What could you sacrifice in order to achieve your goals?*

Examples:
Priority: Write a book Sacrifice: *TV time*
Priority: Get along better with my sister Sacrifice: *Always getting my way*

Priority #1: ________________________________
*Sacrifice(s):*________________________________

Priority #2: ________________________________
*Sacrifice(s):*________________________________

Priority #3: ________________________________
*Sacrifice(s):*________________________________

13

Accept Challenges and Responsibilities

Laziness may appear attractive,
but work gives satisfaction.

—*Anne Frank*

It may sound odd, but one of the best things to avoid in life is avoiding life. A life well lived is filled with responsibilities and challenges, and the way in which you accept these helps determine your integrity and growth. Superstars want the ball when the game is on the line. Once you understand the value of taking responsibility and accepting challenges, your life becomes more exciting and rewarding.

When approached correctly, school and life should challenge you. Sometimes we rationalize avoiding responsibilities and challenges by convincing ourselves that what we are missing isn't a big deal. In school, many students decide that the easiest way to deal with a tough assignment is to simply not do it. I see this happen all too often. (I'm sure you can think of a classmate who fits this profile—hopefully it's not you, but if it is, thankfully, you're reading this chapter!) These types of students don't complete the assignment because doing so would create too much work, stress, or difficulty. This thinking might be partially right—in the short run, skipping an obligation might be easier than performing it, but developing the habit of avoiding problems, challenges, or responsibilities will surely make your life more difficult in the long run.

Even if you can afford to take the easy way out at times, it doesn't mean you should. There are days when I'd rather stay home than go to work, but I still drag myself there. I have sick days that enable me to stay home, but I don't use them on these days because that's not their purpose. Doing so would be avoiding my responsibility, and that's not the right way to live. If I use my sick days on days when I just don't feel like working, I'll be in a tough situation if I ever come down with an illness that keeps me bedridden for a while.

There is an expression that says, "Eighty percent of life is just showing up," and there is much truth to these words. Whether you are faced with tough days, tough tests, or tough conversations in the future, find the positivity and value in doing what needs to be done, even if it seems difficult at the time. Remember that you don't have to do everything yourself; use support networks such as teachers, parents, or friends when you need help. But always show up. Always do what's expected of you, and, better yet, go above and beyond expectations. Become a responsible leader who is willing to tackle any challenge thrown your way. You will amaze yourself and others. That sounds like superstar material to me.

Reflection and Self-Awareness Opportunity

1) *Can you think of a time when you avoided responsibility? If so, what was it?*

2) *What could you have done differently?*

3) *What challenging times or big responsibilities are approaching in your life? How do you plan on dealing with them? How could some of the qualities discussed in other chapters help you?*

14

Ignite Your Internal Motivation

I don't count my sit-ups. I only start counting when it starts hurting because then it really counts. That's what makes you a champion.

—MOHAMMAD ALI

Based on our discussion from last chapter that "eighty percent of life is just showing up," what comprises the other 20 percent? The answer is internal motivation. You see, doing something is all well and good, but doing something well is great. Once you become internally motivated to achieve in your daily pursuits, your potential becomes magical. You become capable of results that others cannot imagine.

Internally driven people go beyond life's minimum requirements. In school, many students struggle to find the internal motivation to push themselves. Work is often completed but not to the best of people's abilities. Countless students dedicate hundreds of hours to developing habits that promote mediocrity. Although doing something is better than doing nothing, it is still problematic. In the case of an assignment, the reason it is problematic is not because grades might suffer (remember, I care little about grades). It is problematic because students are settling for less than what they are capable of achieving. This is a bleak way to live. Doing the minimum amount of work will never render maximum results.

Always strive for magnificence over mediocrity. Outside motivators such as your parents, grades, or teachers may externally spark your performance, but a spark can easily fizzle out. When you ignite the fire that exists within you, you develop a burning desire to succeed. Become a person who accepts challenges, sees things through, and wants to do things well. This is what separates the good from the great, special from spectacular, student from superstar. Once developed, internal motivation transfers to other areas of your life and propels you to future successes. You will begin succeeding not because other people want you to but because you demand the best that exists within yourself.

School is the perfect opportunity to develop your internal motivation because of the wide range of courses you will take. Inevitably you will be expected to do things you like, things you dislike, and things you care little about. If you learn to treat all of these situations equally in terms of finding the 20 percent needed to do all things well, your future self will thank you. For the rest of your life, similar scenarios will occur, be it in your career, family, or other commitments. Tackling all challenges to the best of your ability now will prepare you to accomplish anything in the future.

If being internally motivated becomes part of your identity, you become someone who strives for success. Superstars find it within themselves to put forth their best effort, not matter what. To quote the legendary boxer Muhammad Ali again, "I hated every minute of training, but I said, 'Don't quit. Suffer now and live the rest of your life as a champion.'" With internal motivation you'll go the extra mile, and you'll be so happy and proud of your results that you wouldn't have it any other way. You will live your life like a champion. Ali would be proud.

Reflection and Self-Awareness Opportunity

1) *Think about your past school year. Which statement best reflects your current approach to schoolwork?*

    a) *When I have schoolwork, I try to find a way out of it.*
    b) *When I have schoolwork, I'm just happy to get it over with.*
    c) *When I have schoolwork, I put in effort, but I often know I could do better.*
    d) *When I have schoolwork, I am internally driven to do it well.*

2) *What is an activity in which you usually give your best effort?*

3) *What is an activity in which you typically lack the internal motivation to do it well?*

4) *What might be some benefits of performing both activities you listed to the best of your ability?*

Stage III

Optimize Your Opportunities

Opportunities multiply as they are seized.

—Sun Tzu

Opportunities exist all around you, every day, but you can only capitalize on them if you are aware of them. This stage focuses on recognizing opportunities in school so you can maximize your personal growth.

15

Understand Opportunity Cost

It is in your moments of decision that your destiny is shaped.

—Tony Robbins

The decisions you make create your life. At some point you've likely been told to weigh the pros and cons of each option when making a decision. That's solid advice to follow, but there is another beneficial decision-making strategy known as "opportunity cost." Essentially, opportunity cost means that once you've made a decision, you have also decided to forgo anything else you could have done instead. Understanding this concept can help you make better life decisions.

Opportunity costs can take many forms. One cost that is easy to conceptualize is monetary. Anytime you spend the money you have, you forgo your ability to pay for anything else. Essentially, when you buy something, you have decided that you need or want that item more than any other item on earth. It's an eye-opening concept when you consider your purchases. For example, the opportunity cost of spending all your money on new clothing might be that you cannot save for college or a car. When you consider the opportunity cost of your decisions, you often begin to prioritize your purchases and therefore spend your money more wisely.

Opportunity cost also exists in the form of time. Time is similar to money in that you should always be aware of how you are spending it, but it's more valuable because the qualities you develop and memories you cherish over time are truly priceless. School provides you with valuable time to learn, grow, and create memories. Learning in school extends far beyond course content; it exists in the opportunities you seize and the daily decisions you make. Many students limit their personal growth each day by not considering the opportunity costs of their decisions.

For example, students skip classes for varieties of reasons. What they often do not realize is that the opportunity cost associated with skipping is much more than missing out on that day's lesson. If the only downside of skipping one class was missing course content, it wouldn't be a big deal (you could likely find the information online anyway). But when you analyze the act of skipping itself, especially when it becomes habitual, you begin to understand just how costly it is in terms of developing skills, abilities, and attitudes. Beyond missing the day's lesson, skipping class can result in decreased levels of work ethic, responsibility, persistence, and momentum. These developed qualities are pillars of success that you will need the rest of your life, especially when times get tough. You cannot find these qualities online. You cannot find them by avoiding challenges. By skipping class, you forgo the development of valuable habits and replace them with habits of apathy and avoidance. That's a costly life decision. That's opportunity cost.

Making decisions based on opportunity cost requires a level of maturity because sometimes the decision you make after considering the opportunity cost might not be the most enjoyable decision in the short run. Here are a few examples:

1. **Decision:** Daydream in class.
   Opportunity cost: Develop persistence and learn valuable information.
2. **Decision:** Eat the delicious, greasy meal that is calling your name.
   Opportunity cost: Benefit from healthier food choices, and feel better.
3. **Decision:** Stay up late to watch movies or play video games.
   Opportunity cost: Enjoy a restful sleep and productive tomorrow.

Understanding your own opportunity costs allow you to effectively weigh your options and make more informed decisions. Whether it is the decision to buy clothes, sleep in, fake sick, succumb to peer pressure, or anything else, always try to consider what you're giving up when you make a decision—that's your opportunity cost.

The choices you make are ultimately up to you. Your daily decisions shape your future. Do your best to make smart choices while still living a life you enjoy. There's still a time and place for staying up too late, eating greasy food, and even skipping class (that's right—I said it), but it takes maturity to understand when and how often to do these things. For every decision there is an opportunity cost. If you can save yourself from costly decisions, your time will be well spent and your future will be rich.

Reflection and Self-Awareness Opportunity

1) Think about some of the important decisions you've made in the past year. What were the opportunity costs of those decisions (what weren't you able to do as a result of your decisions)?

Decision #1:
Opportunity Cost:

Decision #2:
Opportunity Cost:

2) After looking at your opportunity costs, are you still happy with the decisions you made?

Decision #1	***Yes***	***No***
Decision #2	***Yes***	***No***

If you answered no, why not?

16

Treasure Your Time

The most precious resource we all have is time.

—STEVE JOBS

Time is incredibly simple yet strangely complex. It's simple because we all get the same twenty-four hours in a day, but it's complex because we don't know when our time will run out. Your life is precious, so your time should be treated as such. Learning to treasure your time will create a life filled with enriching experiences, golden opportunities, and priceless memories.

School is a perfect setting to witness time in action because students choose to use time in so many different ways. There are many active learners who capitalize on numerous opportunities to grow inside and outside the classroom. Watching these students make the most of their time is uplifting. Unfortunately, there are also students who use their time in discouraging fashions. When students view school as merely a place they "have to go," they easily become disengaged. School is by no means a perfect place, and not every element of school will be your forte or favorite, but every minute you spend in school is your time, so try to make a conscious effort to use it wisely.

What you choose to do with your time is what you choose to do with your life.

You won't always optimize your time and that's OK, but be mindful of when those instances happen because simple awareness of how you use your time can reduce how often you misuse your time. When I was in tenth grade, my literature class began with twenty minutes of silent reading. I hated reading, so instead I doodled the symbol of the rap group Wu-Tang Clan and the Nike logo. Did my doodling skills help my future? No. Did I struggle with heavy readings in university? Yes. Was doodling more fun for me at the time than reading? Definitely. If I could go back in time, would I doodle again? Definitely not. I could not doodle my way through life and expect to see results. Life doesn't work that way. Actions determine habits—and I developed the habit of being a distracted reader. It took me years to change my reading habits and become a focused reader. If you spend your time giving your best, you'll be amazed at how much you can accomplish.

Your best habits create your best life. It's my sincere hope that your time in school is filled not only with learning and development, but also with smiles, laughter, fun, and friendship. Life should be fun, and you should do your best to make it that way for yourself and others, but know that those with a superstar-mindset accept that their use of time won't always seem enjoyable. Just because something isn't enjoyable, however, doesn't mean it isn't time well spent. If you want school to serve its full purpose, then you must embrace the times that are not conventionally fun. Learning to struggle your way to success is a tremendous use of time; such moments strengthen and enlighten you. When you have difficulties with an assignment, a course, or a teacher, don't purposely zone out, give up, or settle for less than your best. Embrace these challenging times. Don't give up on conquering the difficult guitar riffs, dance routines, or computer programming languages. Learning to struggle through challenging times is a superstar habit that leads to monumental breakthroughs and moments of brilliance.

Every day you wake up, school day or not, cherish the time you have. It's an opportunity and blessing. Make the most of your minutes because they create the hours that comprise the days of your life. Time really is your most valuable resource. Time that passes will only exist in two forms. It will exist in a new version of you, for better or worse—time allows you the opportunity to develop skills, knowledge, relationships, and attitudes that define you. Or it will exist in memories—but only if memorable moments happen. It's often up to us to create our own memories (keep that in mind next time you play eight straight hours of video games or binge watch two entire seasons of your fourth-favorite show). By treasuring your time you will accomplish more, create positive memories for yourself and others, and live a life that is transformational, happy, and fulfilled. Go and have the time of your life.

Reflection and Self-Awareness Opportunity

1) *Think about how effectively you use your time in school. Write down some ways you could make better use of your time:*

2) *Think about how effectively you use your time outside of school. Write down some ways you could make better use of your time:*

17

Make Reading a Priority

A person who won't read has no advantage over one who can't read.

—Mark Twain

Regardless of your post-high-school plans, reading will be part of your life, so making it a priority now will serve you well. Reading can inform, entertain, and change you in ways that other mediums cannot. Deciding to read is deciding to grow.

Too many students choose to limit their reading. I've taught hundreds of students who, when I asked what they read for fun, would reply that they did not read for fun. They would only read when something was assigned to them in school. When you think about this, it's no wonder they disliked reading. If the only time you pick up a book is after something is assigned to you, then reading will only ever feel like a chore. Nobody likes chores.

Reading is exercise for the mind. It's a lot like running because it too can feel like a chore when you're getting started. When you begin an exercise program and embark on your first run, your pace may be slow and you may lack the stamina to run for a long period before wanting or needing to stop. That's OK because everyone needs to find a starting point that is manageable. You may dislike running initially, but with practice and persistence, your speed and stamina will undoubtedly improve. Over time, positive momentum will build. You'll impress yourself by running at faster paces for longer intervals, and you may even begin to enjoy running so much that you become an avid runner. The same is true for reading. You may be slow in the beginning and may need to start with short intervals, but practice and persistence will improve your reading speed and stamina. This practice will make reading easier and more enjoyable. Eventually, you'll find yourself reading for fun and become an avid reader. Dedicated practice always leads to improved results.

Reading doesn't have to be a huge commitment. You don't have to wake up at six o'clock and read for a few hours like those admirable runners who leave ten miles in their dust before sunrise. Your reading can be fifteen minutes before bed, on the bus, whenever and wherever. What you read can come from anywhere: books, newspapers, or online. Just make sure that what you read has some substance—for instance, social media or online shopping isn't focused reading, so it won't provide you with the same benefits as a book or article. When you find the right book (it may take time, but you will), those fifteen minutes you allotted for reading time will turn into hours where you are living inside the book.

To make reading most fun, read based on your personal interests. Books can be an escape to freedom, a time to unwind, or a challenge to the mind. Plus, it's a healthy habit. If you read what interests you, eventually the obligation to read will transform into an opportunity. Books can challenge your thinking by broadening your perspective. They can allow you to spend time with legends, from business icons such as Steve Jobs or Oprah Winfrey, to beloved humanitarians such as Princess Diana or Nelson Mandela, to celebrated superstars such as Beyoncé or Bono. So much can be learned from our world's most fascinating people. Books are a gateway into the planet's most interesting minds.

Once you become an avid reader, continue broadening your own mind by selecting different authors, styles, and genres. There are so many phenomenal novels, biographies, memoirs, and other types of books filled with ideas you don't yet know exist. Oprah Winfrey explained this well when she said, "Books were my pass to personal freedom. I learned to read at age three, and soon discovered that there was a whole world to conquer beyond our farm in Mississippi." Reading can help you see and understand the world and its possibilities from unimaginable perspectives.

Reading will take you places, literally and figuratively. Carving out some regular reading time will make you more intelligent, articulate, and open-minded. Sacrifice some TV time. Find a relaxing space. Put down your phone and pick up a book. And keep picking up books. By learning to embrace reading, you'll fill your mind with words of wisdom and make your own life's story even better.

PS: Make reading part of your summer vacation. Studies show that you'll be much better off when school starts up again. Also, without school obligations, summer is the perfect time to read books of your choice.

Reflection and Self-Awareness Opportunity

1) *Circle the statement that best applies to your current reading habits:*
    a) *I am an avid reader, and I read a wide selection of books.*
    b) *I am an avid reader, but I could widen my selection of books.*
    c) *I read sometimes, and I'm eager to read more.*
    d) *I read sometimes, but not as much as I should.*
    e) *I don't read as often as I should. I'm shocked I'm even reading this book!*

If you circled C, D, or E, what could you do to improve your reading lifestyle?

2) *List some genres that you don't currently read but might be of interest to you.*

Ex: Nonfiction, fiction, biographies, history, war, graphic novels, poetry, etc.

3) *Write down two people you are interested in learning more about. Do an online search to see if there are books written by them or about them.*

18

Value Volunteerism

The best way to find yourself is to lose yourself in the service of others.

—MAHATMA GANDHI

There is no bigger superstar than someone who helps others. Life can be crazy busy, so it's admirable when people donate their own time for a cause they find worthy. Volunteers make society a better place. Think about your own life. It's likely that at some point you've been involved in a group or activity that was led by a volunteer. Maybe a certain individual stands out as a role model or mentor. Valuing volunteerism is an easy way to improve your life and the lives of others.

You will learn more about yourself through volunteering. Many teenagers leave high school still not knowing what they want to do in their lives. This is normal, but one reason this is the case is because teenagers have yet to experience much for themselves. They've only done what they've had to do. Volunteering allows you to gain new experiences that might lead you down new roads and open up doors to places you'll love. Volunteering can help you find a passion for living and giving—a dynamic combination.

Everyone has various life commitments, so it's easy to rationalize not having time to volunteer. You're correct in thinking that volunteering takes up time in an already busy life, but it can actually save you time by narrowing your interests, which can help you determine future pathways for life. I knew that I was interested in becoming a teacher, but after I volunteered at a camp filled with elementary school children, it didn't take me long to cross elementary school teacher off the list. Volunteering broadened my perspective yet narrowed my focus. Regardless of whether your volunteer experience is positive or negative at the time, it will tell you something about yourself. Learning about yourself is always positive.

We live in a competitive world, and volunteering as a teenager can help you gain a competitive edge. It can help you stand out among your competition in a job, college, or scholarship application. Volunteer experience shows that you are:

- Caring (you give up your own time for a cause that is important to you).
- Hard-working (if you are willing to work for no money, imagine how hard you will work when you are getting paid).
- Mature (it takes maturity to voluntarily do something for others).

Employers and educational institutions love to see these traits on an application, and voluntary service to others demonstrates them brilliantly.

It's so important to help others, and what's neat is that when you help others, you also help yourself. When I reflect on the thousands of hours I have spent coaching, I feel happy and proud. Happy because it's something I enjoy—I've been places, developed relationships, and shared in experiences that I'll never forget. And proud because I dedicated my own time to help others. Many coaches did the same for me when I was growing up, and I'm so grateful they did. It feels good to give back. Too often we get so caught up in receiving things that we forget how good it feels to give. Helping others is always a worthwhile endeavor. Remember, the world needs you to care about it.

Volunteering doesn't have to be a big undertaking; in fact, you will probably want to start small. Your school community is a great place to begin volunteering because it will connect you to the school in a way that classwork cannot. When school becomes a place where you take in knowledge but also give something back, your life as a student will have more purpose. There are likely clubs or events that need different levels of volunteers. Find something that interests you and give it a try. It could be something that directly affects a small group of people in your school or something that raises awareness for a worthy cause in a different country. If you can't find anything of interest, get some friends together and create your own volunteer group. Everyone brings something unique to the table. Find a way to share your strengths and passions with the world in a way that gives back.

My only warning is that volunteering might lead you down unexpected paths, so be careful. If you start volunteering, next thing you know you will learn a whole lot about yourself, make new friends, gain valuable experience, stand out among your competition, find your passion, help others, and feel proud. That is a lot to have on your plate, but it's a pretty tasty dish, like my grandfather's spaghetti. I'd volunteer to eat that any day.

Reflection and Self-Awareness Opportunity

1) *What is an activity/event you have done in the past that relied on volunteers? Do you think the volunteers were important? Why or why not?*

2) *For what type of activity/event do you think you might like to volunteer? What are some benefits that could result from the experience?*

3) *If you currently volunteer or have volunteered in the past, how did it make you feel?*

19

Learn Effective Listening

When you talk, you are only repeating what you already know; but when you listen, you may learn something new.

—DALAI LAMA

Your life becomes easier when you are an effective communicator. Depending on your personality, your willingness to speak in public settings may vary (although I do encourage you to let your voice be heard—too much excellent insight goes unheard in this world), but your willingness to listen has much less to do with your personality and more to do with your character. Being an effective listener involves being fully present in a given moment, which is a choice. If you can become an effective listener, you will drastically improve your capacity to learn.

Avid listening leads to avid learning; however, advice about how to listen effectively is often neglected. Teachers readily mention tips for speaking or delivering a powerful presentation, but when it's time for listening, you simply hear, "OK, class, everyone listen up!" Or the ever-so-detailed advice "Eyes and ears up here, everybody." Listening is a skill we use every day, so it's worth knowing how to do it well.

The toughest part of effective listening is making a conscious effort to do so. School offers you a chance to hone your listening skills in various settings with a variety of audiences. If you follow these five simple tips, you'll be set:

1. *Make eye contact with the speaker* (don't stare, though—that's just creepy). Making eye contact sounds obvious, but so many people struggle with this. I'm sure you can picture the students in your class who always have their heads on their desks. Or how about people who are glued to their phones? If you ever find yourself doing these things, remember that you are always part of something bigger, remember that you are a class act, and ask yourself how you'd feel if the whole class did that while you were speaking. Making eye contact keeps your focus on the speaker, thus improving your ability to listen and learn.
2. *Have a posture that shows you are interested* (even if you're not interested). When someone is speaking to you, don't slouch, put your head down, or lean way back in your chair. Be upright, but not uptight. Being appropriately comfortable improves your alertness and puts the speaker at ease. Plus, it's the polite thing to do.
3. *Be an active listener.* Using nonverbal cues such as nodding, smiling, laughing, or frowning at appropriate times show that you are engaged. (Doing these things at the wrong times can make for some awkward situations.) Also, asking questions or clarifying important points helps keeps you involved in the communication process. Active listening makes you listen more closely.
4. *Don't be thinking when you should be listening.* If a speaker makes a point that you disagree with or that you would like to comment on, don't immediately start planning a rebuttal

or comment in your head. When you start thinking, you stop listening and could therefore miss the rest of the speaker's point, which could be valuable information. Listen to understand. Always hear the speaker out completely before turning your attention to your own thoughts. You will get your chance to speak, and by listening the entire time, you'll have more information to draw from when forming your points.

5. *Take notes* (when necessary or appropriate). If you use this tip on a first date, it will likely also be your last date with that person. If you use this tip in class, it can be a big help. Jotting down key points from a speaker can help you retain information. It can also keep you on task and refrain you from thinking too much when you should be listening. Then, when it's time to speak, you can refer to your notes to help gather your own thoughts. Instead of trying to remember key points, you'll have important information written down that you can review. Plus, if you plan on attending postsecondary school, this will be expected of you, so you might as well begin practicing now.

You'll notice from these tips that effective listening involves more than just your ears; it's about being fully present in a given moment—such a superstar quality. School provides many opportunities to practice listening, so make your time meaningful. Listening skills translate from individual to group situations, formal to informal, and although they are not complex, they do require discipline and a willingness to actively participate in a conversation even when it is not you doing the talking. If you become a more effective listener, you will absorb more information and enjoy more enriching dialogue. The more information you absorb, the more you have to draw from. Your willingness to listen speaks volumes about your willingness to learn. If you learn to listen, you'll turn your life up a notch.

Reflection and Self-Awareness Opportunity

1) *Rate yourself out of 5 for the following statements:*
Legend: 1=Never 2=Rarely 3=Sometimes 4=Often 5=Always
I make eye contact when someone is speaking to me in a group setting.
1 2 3 4 5
My posture conveys that I am an engaged listener.
1 2 3 4 5
I use nonverbal cues (nodding, smiling, etc.) to show that I am an active listener.
1 2 3 4 5
I make sure I listen until the speaker is finished before I begin constructing my own thoughts.
1 2 3 4 5
When appropriate, I jot down key points that a speaker mentions.
1 2 3 4 5

2) *Try to employ the chapter tips about effective listening during your next class. Write about what you noticed afterward.*

20

Step Out of Your Comfort Zone

The biggest risk is not taking any risk...In a world that is changing so quickly, the only strategy that is guaranteed to fail is not taking risks.

—MARK ZUCKERBERG

If life were filled with doors of opportunity, everyone would walk on through to success, but life is not that easy. Instead, the saying we use is "a window of opportunity"; in order to capitalize on it, you must be willing to get uncomfortable and climb through. Life experiences that bring the biggest opportunities and rewards are often those in which we must step out of our respective comfort zones. Voluntarily taking some personal risks is a courageous act that pushes boundaries, brings development, and drives success.

School is supposed to challenge you, but sometimes it is up to you to create the challenge. For instance, high school provides you with opportunities to enroll in subjects or programs about which you might know little or nothing. Don't immediately dismiss these options. Too many students opt for courses that are in their comfort zones instead of using the opportunity to expand their horizons. I, regretfully, was one of those students. In my case, a culinary course and a carpentry course were offered at my high school, but I opted for physical education courses, which were more in my comfort zone. I was already exceptionally active outside of school, so I didn't need the daily physical activity in school, but I knew I'd find the courses easy. Now, at age thirty-two, I'm still physically active (I would have been regardless of whether or not I took phys ed courses), but my culinary and carpentry skills remain minimal. Instead of taking a personal challenge in school, I settled for being comfortable and missed an opportunity to develop. I won't go so far as to say I made the wrong choice by taking phys ed instead of the others (there's a lot to be said for following your interests and passion), but I didn't give those other options the consideration I should have. Who knows—maybe I would have become a world-famous chef! Hors d'oeuvres, anyone?

Beyond the classroom there are many opportunities in school to take personal risks, so dare to explore. Famed explorer Christopher Columbus said, "You can never cross the ocean unless you have the courage to lose sight of the shore." Believe in your ability to tread in unknown waters and face new challenges. These actions often lead to life-changing discoveries. Audition for the play and try out for the team. Ask that special someone on a date (you know who I'm talking about). Share your ideas with others. Make new friends and try new foods. Challenge your work ethic and learn to struggle. Explore your creative side. The more you step into the unknown, the more you will know. You'll never realize what amazing things you're capable of doing unless you try doing amazing things.

Stepping out of your comfort zone is not easy, but the personal growth you experience as a result makes it worthwhile. Although taking a personal risk might be scary initially, what's neat is that the more you do it, the easier it becomes. Your comfort zone expands every time you challenge yourself. This is good because life will challenge you. You will find yourself in future situations (often unwillingly) where you feel uncomfortable, anxious, or insecure. Voluntarily living bits of your life outside your comfort zone now will improve your ability to handle the unexpected challenges that will inevitably come your way. The bottom line is that life's epic moments rarely occur inside comfort zones. Unfamiliar territories and uncomfortable challenges create unforgettable experiences and unprecedented growth.

Note: Too much of anything is bad, including taking on too many challenging endeavors at once. Don't push yourself too far. First, take smart risks only—don't jeopardize your safety or your future by taking unsafe risks. Your life is too valuable. Second, balance is key. Sometimes staying in your comfort zone is the best move. For instance, if you already have a challenging course load, then choosing a less challenging elective might be the right decision. Find a balance that works for you.

Reflection and Self-Awareness Opportunity

1) *How often do you step out of your comfort zone?*
    a) *I never step out of my comfort zone.*
    b) *I rarely step out of my comfort zone.*
    c) *I sometimes step out of my comfort zone.*
    d) *I often step out of my comfort zone.*
    e) *I step out of my comfort zone whenever I get the chance.*

2) *Write down an opportunity you have to step out of your comfort zone. What might be some potential benefits of this experience?*

21

Never Stop Learning

Once you stop learning, you start dying.

—ALBERT EINSTEIN

From her nursing home, my eighty-seven-year-old grandmother continues to model advice she gave me when I began my teaching career. A retired teacher herself, she was adamant that even though my job was now to teach others, it was imperative that I never stop learning. My nannie's body is slowly deteriorating, but her mind is still vibrant. She reads. She listens and asks questions during our conversations, and she tackles new challenges every day. She is still learning, and it's inspiring. Lifelong learning is vital to personal growth and a life well lived.

In order to live a life where learning is continuous, you must be teachable. Once you develop teachable characteristics, your learning will never stop. Teachable people share the following three characteristics:

They accept that learning is a challenge. Wanting to know what you don't yet know is a challenging opportunity. For some students, unknown possibilities can frustrate and freeze learning, but for teachable students, these same unknowns fuel learning. If you view learning as a challenge, you become more prone to doing what it takes to learn. Instead of crumbling when learning gets tough, you will have the work ethic, inquisitiveness, and persistence necessary to succeed. Superstar artist Pablo Picasso said, “I’m always doing that which I can not do, in order that I may learn how to do it.” Challenging yourself to learn helps you learn more. Knowledge is power.

They are optimistic about learning. Teachable people recognize that learning can happen anytime, anywhere, from anyone. For a variety of unfortunate reasons, many students bring pessimistic attitudes into the classroom. You might believe you have good reasons for such an attitude, and who am I to tell you you’re wrong? Heck, you might be right; people often come from challenging circumstances that are beyond their control. But remember that the attitude you bring into a learning environment is a personal choice you make each day. It is often the mind-set, and not the mind, that keeps a person from learning. Many students stand on similar footing from an intellectual standpoint, yet the amount they learn in classes varies tremendously. Choosing a positive attitude that views each day as an opportunity to learn will enrich your learning experiences and make your life more fulfilling.

They never give up. For teachable people, failure is part of their repertoire; it’s sometimes necessary but always temporary. When you can accept disappointment and criticism yet push forward, you learn. When you can own your mistakes and keep going, you learn. When you can look yourself in the mirror and know that you are capable of changing, even though it may be difficult, you learn. Teachable people never give up; it’s during tough times that they often learn the most.

Learning experiences extend far beyond the walls of a classroom. They exist on the fields and courts. At the musician’s and painter’s studio. In the pages you read and shows you watch. During times of love or heartbreak, joy or sadness, life will never stop presenting learning opportunities that foster growth. Some will be easy to recognize (open your math book to page 223) and others more difficult (the death of a loved one might teach you to cherish your life and relationships more closely). Learning will happen all around you for the rest of your days. It is said that with age comes wisdom, but this is only true if you are willing to learn over time. The more teachable characteristics you possess, the wiser you will become.

Note: With my grandmother on my mind, I'm reminded of something. You can gain so much insight from your elders. Older people have knowledge and experiences that are invaluable—they've learned, experienced successes, and made mistakes. Spend some time with them, ask them questions, and pick their brains (not literally; that's gross zombie stuff). They often love to share their life experiences with the younger generation. It's a win-win. Plus, you and I will be them someday if we are lucky. I'm sure we will appreciate the conversations, too.

One more side note about my nannie—she passed away shortly after I had written this chapter. I was fortunate enough to spend her last few days with her. She was a widow who lived in a nursing home, and up until the moment she died she was still as loving, kind, and grateful as ever. She taught me that when such qualities are part of your character, they never leave. That's a lesson worth learning. Superstars are truly everywhere.

Reflection and Self-Awareness Opportunity

1) *Rate yourself out of 5 for the following statements to evaluate your teachable characteristics:*

   Legend: 1=Never 2=Rarely 3=Sometimes 4=Often 5=Always

   a) *I rise to challenges that are placed before me.*

      1 2 3 4 5

   b) *I view an experience as an opportunity to learn.*

      1 2 3 4 5

   c) *I view failure as an opportunity to come back stronger.*

      1 2 3 4 5

2) *Circle the teachable characteristic that you could improve upon the most:*

   a) *Accepting that learning is a challenge*
   b) *Being optimistic about learning*
   c) *Never giving up*

Stage IV

Become the Leader of Your Life

Change will not come if we wait for some other person or some other time. We are the ones we've been waiting for. We are the change that we seek.

—Barack Obama

The most successful leaders understand that positive change is impossible without an internal willingness to improve. This stage focuses on developing superstar qualities that allow you to best serve yourself and others.

22

Believe in Yourself

The first step is you have to say that you can.

—Will Smith

At your age, it is amazing how much potential and opportunity you have. For instance, right now there is a future prime minister or president who is roughly your age. I hope she or he is reading this book (that would be cool). It might be you (that would be cooler). It's neat to think about that stuff, and I hope you do think about that stuff. Your future is unwritten, so do your best to write an epic life story. Chase your dreams, face your fears, and, most importantly, always believe in yourself. How much you believe will greatly determine how much you achieve.

Sometimes life is all about confidence. In my classes, many students despise delivering presentations because they are nervous of what their peers will think. Public speaking is a real fear for many. I remember one student, Kenneth, who delivered a presentation in my class, and in all honesty, it was bad. He hadn't rehearsed, he looked nervous, and he spoke quietly and cautiously. He did pretty much everything you're not supposed to do when presenting. His performance wasn't entirely shocking, though, because Kenneth had become accustomed to failing assignments. He had no confidence when it came to school.

After his presentation, I asked him how he thought he had done. His response was "Not good. I suck at presenting." The first part of his analysis was true—his presentation wasn't good. The second part, however, was where the real problem existed. "I suck at presenting" really meant "I don't believe in myself."

You will struggle with any task when you don't believe in yourself. It's good to be self-aware and realistic about your weaknesses, but be careful that you don't sell yourself short. We all have weaknesses, but that doesn't mean they can't one day be strengths. We all have doubts, but that doesn't mean they can't one day be beliefs. We all have dreams, but that doesn't mean they can't one day be realities. Sometimes the real reason we are unsuccessful is simply because we lack the confidence to succeed.

I knew Kenneth was capable of better work than what he had produced because I had witnessed him interact with classmates. He was funny, interesting, and outgoing—all elements of a talented presenter—so I wasn't buying his story that he "sucked at presenting." When I pointed out Kenneth's strengths to him, he sheepishly smiled and reluctantly agreed with me. By realizing his capabilities, his mind-set changed from "I suck at everything I do in school" to "I have skills and talents." He was building self-confidence.

Kenneth shocked the class with his next presentation. He was the same person physically; he wasn't any smarter than before but the way he believed in himself transformed his entire demeanor. His presentation was so good (and so shocking) that he received a standing ovation from his classmates. His success in that moment spread confidence into other parts of his life. He improved his work ethic, became more responsible, and was a happier individual—all because he believed in himself.

Whether it is school, music, sports, or anything else, never diminish your self-worth. Self-confidence improves your mind-set, which helps you find the qualities needed to overcome obstacles, step out of your comfort zone, and shock the world. Celebrate your strengths and work on your weaknesses. View disappointments as character builders and come back stronger. Surround yourself with people who motivate you and believe in you. Get to know your inner superstar. Believing in yourself will make your life unbelievable.

PS: On days when you are lacking self-confidence and feel as if no one believes in you, remember that I do (I wouldn't have written this book if I didn't). It's always good to have a fan club.

Reflection and Self-Awareness Opportunity

1) *Write down two of your best qualities. Remember not to sell yourself short. You are a superstar!*

2) *In BIG PRINT, write something that you'd love to accomplish. Remember to dream big. If you believe it, you can achieve it.*

23

Don't Let Your Past Define You

I've failed over and over and over again in my life... and that is why I succeed.

—MICHAEL JORDAN

Sometimes there is nothing better than a fresh start. In my school, student grades range from ten through twelve, and although I teach all grades, my favorite classes are first-semester tenth-grade classes because it's a new school year, a new environment, and a new life chapter for students. But although everyone has a fresh start, it doesn't mean everyone starts fresh. Some people let their pasts limit their futures. Every day can serve as a new beginning for your life's path because it is an opportunity for change, growth, and greatness. Don't let your yesterdays ruin your todays and restrict your tomorrows.

Even when we're given a new opportunity, it is understandable why we might fill a clean slate with negativity right off the bat. History has a way of repeating itself, and negativity is often derived from bad past experiences. For instance, if you struggled with various aspects of school in the past, assuming that these negative experiences will continue into the coming school year might be logical. Although this thinking is understandable, it doesn't mean it is the right mind-set. Living in the past makes it difficult to move forward. Why let your thoughts limit your potential? It's true that your past has shaped who you are today, so it's important to acknowledge the past, but it does not define who you can become. Part of your personal growth is adapting and, in some instances, reinventing yourself.

The world's most successful people use their pasts as building blocks instead of roadblocks. Superstar athlete Michael Jordan, arguably the greatest basketball player of all time, was cut from his high-school varsity basketball team. If he had classified himself as a second-tier athlete after being cut, he would have never worked on his skills enough to become the sports legend he is today (and I would have never had the coolest sneakers in fourth grade). Another example is famous author J. K. Rowling. Numerous publishers initially rejected her world-renowned story of Harry Potter. If she had let those rejections define her as an author, she would have never found the resilience and persistence to bring her international best-selling novel series to fruition (and I would have never learned the meaning of a muggle). In both cases, their pasts didn't define who they were. Instead, their pasts helped create who they would become.

It's difficult to fathom the past struggles of MJ and JK given their iconic successes, but their stories show how legends are made and not born. Remember that Michael Jordan or J. K. Rowling were once teenagers just like you. You, too, can become a superstar in life. You can be the best version of yourself, and for that there are no comparisons. Your success truly knows no boundaries.

Every day provides an opportunity to redefine your life. Just because you were a bad student (or friend, or anything else) last year, last week, or even today, doesn't mean you must label yourself as such moving forward. Instead of focusing on your past, envision the person you'd like to be in the future. Use this vision to guide your present actions. Actions that are based on becoming the person you define yourself to be will give you a renewed sense of purpose and drive, which will make achieving your goals easier. Remember, changing your outlook on life can change your life. On the flip side, if you have done well in the past, it doesn't mean you'll continue to do well without putting in the effort. The future always allows for improvements, but it also allows for declines—which one occurs is often up to you. Not letting your past define you is a wonderful present to give your future. See what I did there? Past, present, future? Well, I'm impressed anyway. Becoming legendary begins today.

Note: Although your past cannot define your future, the consequences of past actions can sometimes limit your future, so always be aware of the decisions you make. Be smart.

Reflection and Self-Awareness Opportunity

1) *What is something from your past that you feel might define you in a negative way? Is that how you define yourself now?*

If it is, how would your prefer to define yourself? What daily actions could help you reinvent yourself and focus on your present opportunities instead of your past?

24

Be Better Than Yesterday

The day you think there are no improvements to be made is a sad day for anyone.

—Lionel Messi

A friend of mine shared a picture online of a whiteboard that hung in her fourteen-year-old son's room. On this board he had written the quote "The only person you should try to be better than is the person you were yesterday." I had heard or read this expression many times throughout my life to the point where it seemed cliché, but when I processed that this teenager had purposefully put it on his whiteboard, it suddenly connected with me. I thought, if this fourteen-year-old actually commits to living by this quote, he is going to have one phenomenal life.

Your teenage years are transformative times when your daily actions are critical to your development and identity. Seeing students develop from timid teenagers into confident young adults ready to take on the world is the uplifting, sunny side of student transformation. Unfortunately, there is also a heartbreaking, darker side. Every year, teenagers with a world of potential go from having so much promise to so little hope. Students often don't realize that their daily decisions are creating their negative transformation. Their downward spiral, whether it is because of social issues, personal issues, drug issues, or any other reason, often begins with small daily actions that snowball exponentially over time. By taking time to evaluate your life and its path on a daily basis, you can help ensure that you are living a life you love.

Trying to be better than you were yesterday speaks of gradual improvement. The truth is, life will not always feel like constant improvement. You (and everyone else on earth) will endure bad days when you do and say things you regret, use poor judgment, and more. Obviously you want to limit these days, but they are inevitable. So, more specifically, you want to avoid having a number of these days consecutively. By asking yourself the question "Am I a better person than I was yesterday?" you can limit your potential losing streaks and prolong your winning streaks. With enough daily wins, you become an all-star.

There are different ways to approach the question "Am I a better person than I was yesterday?" You can assess your overall self in a general sense (am I a better person?), or you can break down your gradual transformation into the various components of your life (are you a better son or daughter, brother or sister, friend, student, teammate, band member, role model, etc.?). You can also focus on personal traits as a way to assess your gradual transformation (are you more patient, social, disciplined, positive, better at listening, etc.?). A daily check-up will keep you on track and inspire you to improve your life.

Trying only to be better than yourself also keeps you from comparing yourself to others. As a society we get so caught up in the lives of others that it hinders our ability to appreciate our own lives. When comparing ourselves to others, we often choose to compare in terms of what we don't have. We fill our minds with what we perceive to be wrong or missing in our lives. We generate self-pity and dejection instead of self-assessment and reflection. This is damaging because self-assessment allows us to reflect and realize how fortunate, gifted, and blessed we are in so many ways. School can sometimes become a hot zone for comparisons. It's easy to get caught up in comparing yourself to others in grades, social status, looks, talents, or anything else. These comparisons are sometimes helpful and healthy when they serve as motivators, but too often they are physically, mentally, and emotionally draining. Take control of your future by focusing on what you can control—your own life.

Whether you get every break in the world or you have all odds stacked against you, it is always up to you to make the most of your life. A life well lived is composed of worthwhile daily actions. You deserve your best attitude and effort. Your life is what you make of it, so why not try to make it better every day? If you do, you'll live an amazing life, one day at a time.

Reflection and Self-Awareness Opportunity

1) *Write down two ways that you could become a better person than you were yesterday (or in the recent past). Explain what daily actions you would take in order to improve.*

   1.

   Actions:

   2.

   Actions:

2) *Write down a time when you have compared yourself to others. How did it make you feel? What could you have done instead?*

25

"Don't Worry, Be Happy"

There is no path to happiness; happiness is the path.

—BUDDHA

Happiness is one of life's finest feelings, yet too often we do not let it into our lives. My younger brother used to quote the title of Bobby McFerrin's famous song "Don't Worry, Be Happy" at the end of every e-mail he sent. One day I asked him why he had chosen that quote, and he said, "Everyone can understand it, everyone can put it into practice, and it's a good general mantra." I loved his answer. Everyone can be happy because happiness is an attitude, and your attitude is a personal choice. Choosing to live a happy life will lead you down a path of positivity, making every day more remarkable.

Let's get this straight: focusing on happiness does not mean that you will always be happy, but it does mean that you will be happy more. Your worries and your happiness, along with a whack of other feelings, are generated from within. The quote "Don't worry, be happy" acknowledges that tough times exist (the "don't worry" part), but it emphasizes how you can control the way in which negative experiences affect you (the "be happy" part). Consciously deciding to focus on the good that exists in your life makes it easier to deal with the bad.

We often become so stressed that we forget about happiness. There is no denying that school and your teenage years in general bring stressful and anxious times (a.k.a. worry). You have so much to consider, ranging from social situations and financial issues, to academic expectations and future considerations. These times of stress are going to continue to exist for your entire life, just in different manners, so it is important to not let these worries control you. This doesn't mean you should neglect responsibility; it means you should find the positives that exist in whatever life throws at you, whether it seems positive at the time or not. Happiness can exist in almost any situation with the right mind-set. For instance, school isn't always the most fun place, but instead of viewing school as somewhere you have to go (negative outlook), view it as a place you get to go (positive outlook—formal education is a privilege that millions of teenagers around the world do not get to experience). If you dislike a class, focus on the positive opportunity to be with your friends. If there aren't friends in your class, focus on the positive opportunity to concentrate on learning and make new friends. A shift in your mind-set can be all it takes to turn unhappiness into happiness.

Choosing to focus on happiness will improve your life in more ways than you realize. You'll laugh and smile more. You'll do more of what you love. You'll see more value and meaning in every experience. You'll give more to others and forgive more easily. You'll develop closer relationships and bounce back more quickly. You'll become a more grateful person. What's neat is that all these benefits of happiness also bring more happiness, so the effects of focusing on positivity will multiply to create an increasingly enriching life.

Remember, perception is reality, and happiness is a perspective. It's so important to spend time doing what makes you happy, but know that with the right mind-set you can always make happiness a reality. At times, life will still be unfair, no fun, and downright cruel, but living by the simple mantra "Don't worry, be happy" will shift your focus from negative to positive no matter what is thrown your way. With a positive mind-set, the happy moments in life will become more enjoyable. The bad moments will still happen; they just won't seem as bad. And that's good. That's something to be happy about. I'm doing my happy dance right now.

Reflection and Self-Awareness Opportunity

1) ***Don't Worry**—In general, how much time do you spend worrying about things you can't control?*

   a) *I spend way too much time worrying about everything.*
   b) *Even though I try not to, I often find myself worrying.*
   c) *I typically don't worry about things I can't control.*
   d) *I never worry about things I can't control.*

2) ***Be Happy**—In general, how happy are you?*

   a) *I am generally an unhappy person.*
   b) *I am up and down when it comes to happiness.*
   c) *I am generally a happy person.*

3) *Write down three things in your life for which you are grateful:*

   1.

   2.

   3.

Smile! That list is something to be happy about.

4) *Now shift your focus. Write down one thing that would typically make you unhappy and try to find the positive that exists in it.*

Example:

Negative: Got into an argument with my close friend.

Positive: Had a chance to talk with her and make our friendship stronger.

Negative:

Positive:

26

Be True to You

Today you are you. That is truer than true. There is no one alive who is youer than you.

—DR. SEUSS

Only those who remain true to themselves live their finest life. Being yourself is not always easy, but it is essential if you want to perform at your highest levels. The sooner you realize how special you are, the sooner you'll be able to share your unique awesomeness with the world.

You cannot be yourself when you are living in the minds of others. Too often we concern ourselves with what others will think of our personality, style, or abilities that we begin to think and make decisions based on others' thoughts instead of our own. This leads to overanalyzing ourselves, which creates doubt and insecurity. These negative thoughts can alter our behavior and make us act in unauthentic ways. It will serve you well in school and throughout your life to worry less about fitting in and more about standing out.

Everyone is different, and that's what makes everyone special. Superstar musician John Lennon explained it simply when he said,

"It's not weird to be weird," so celebrate your own weird self. The people who really matter will love you, and more importantly, you'll love yourself. The Leaning Tower of Pisa is a beloved landmark because it is crooked. Embrace your imperfections—they are what make you unique. Unleash your quirky personality—it's a rare gift. Show off your strengths—they are what allow you to best serve yourself and others. Acknowledge your weaknesses—they can transform into strengths only once identified. You are a one-of-a-kind, extraordinary gem. There truly is no one else in the world like you. Having the courage to be the most positive, authentic, and ever-improving version of yourself is the greatest gift you can give the world.

Life is a constant exploration of the self, and the more aware you become of your daily actions, the easier it is to learn about yourself. Live an involved life; participating in experiences that complement your values will help you find your passion and allow you to shine brightest. Surround yourself with people who lift your spirits; sharing time with true friends and loved ones will create an environment that enables you to act in your most authentic ways. Find some downtime to reflect daily; in a world full of distraction, carving out ten minutes of alone time to think about your attitude and actions makes it easier to evaluate your life's direction. Silence allows you to relax, de-stress, and ensure that important daily decisions, such as the people with whom you surround yourself or how you are choosing to use your time, are meaningful for you. The more you consciously fill your days with people and experiences you enjoy, the more you'll enjoy being yourself. Living meaningful days, over time, becomes living an inspired life.

Note: In order to be your best self in mind, body, and spirit, you must take care of yourself. *Find time for physical activity*—daily exercise will boost your energy, sharpen your focus, and have you feeling awesome. *Get enough sleep*—you can't produce at superstar levels without proper rest. *Fuel your body with real food*—developing superstar qualities takes energy; eating well will ensure that you have enough fuel to go the extra mile. This whole book is about setting you up for success, so stay true to yourself by preparing your body and mind for a healthy and happy life.

Reflection and Self-Awareness Opportunity

1) *Which statement best describes how authentic you are in your social groups?*
   a) *I always find it hard to be myself.*
   b) *I sometimes find it hard to be myself.*
   c) *I am usually comfortable being myself.*
   d) *I am always comfortable being myself.*

If you answered A or B, what could you try doing to improve this situation?

2) *Take a few minutes, distraction free, to think about your recent attitudes and actions. What do they reveal about your life and its current direction?*

3) *How prepared is your mind, body, and spirit for a life well lived? Which components of a healthy lifestyle could you improve upon?*
   a) *Physical activity*
   b) *Sleep*
   c) *Downtime (reflection)*

Try creating a SMART goal, along with actions, for any areas you identified. Refer to Chapter 7 for help with this activity.

27

Be Inspirational

Each person must live their life as a model for others.

—Rosa Parks

An inspired life is a life with purpose. What inspires us can come from anywhere: nature, art, music, athletics, or anything else can motivate us to act in astonishing ways and accomplish amazing feats. Observing other people is also a tremendous source of inspiration; the actions, attitudes, or attributes of certain individuals are often inspirational. Whether it is a celebrity, friend, family member, or stranger, I'm sure somebody lives life in a way that inspires you. Inspiration is a beautiful gift; it is great to receive, but giving the gift of inspiration to others is even more gratifying.

Daily commitment to living your best life will make you inspirational. You do not have to be famous or do something extravagant. One act of kindness, courage, or compassion can make others want to better themselves because of you. Your actions just might be the inspiration someone needs—you never know what struggles people are facing in their own lives. To quote civil rights activist Maya Angelou,

"Try to be a rainbow in someone else's cloud," and let your actions bring light and beauty into someone's world.

School offers you a multitude of opportunities to inspire others every day. You can act as an inspiration by:

- Trying your best
- Stepping out of your comfort zone
- Standing up for a person or cause
- Staying true to yourself
- Packing a healthy lunch
- Living an active lifestyle
- Pursuing your passion
- Helping others

And the list goes on. Living your life as a model for others makes you a leader by example. This is so important because ten to twenty years from now, your generation will lead the world. You heard that right: lead the world. Your decisions and actions will guide and shape your life and the lives of others. It's a big responsibility, but it should not scare you. It should excite you. It's an inspirational opportunity.

Giving your best effort in life will bring out the best in others, who will then go on to inspire even more people. Imagine what could be accomplished if the whole world lived as a model for others. Thinking about it gives me chills. Inspiration ignites effort which creates greatness, and that's what the world needs. The world cannot survive and thrive without inspirational people.

Remember that success in school or life is not truly measured by the mark you receive, but it can be measured by the mark you leave. Continue to find inspirational motivation from others, but show your gratitude by living in a way that inspires those around you. If you learn to act as an inspiration now, not only will you propel yourself to prosperity, but you will also live a fulfilled life knowing that you made a difference in the lives of others. You'll give others the gift of inspiration. That is a superstar quality if there ever was one.

Reflection and Self-Awareness Opportunity

1) *Think of someone who has been inspirational in your life. What qualities or actions do you admire about that person?*

2) *When you think of your life now, could any of your daily actions inspire others?*
   Yes *No* *Sometimes*

If yes, keep it up! Write down your best actions so you continue to lead by example and inspire others:

If you answered no or sometimes, write down a change you could make in your life that could also inspire others to improve. Refer to the list in the chapter for ideas.

28

Create Positive Change

The secret of change is to focus all of your energy, not on fighting the old, but on building the new.

—SOCRATES

Be excited for the changes you can make in your life, because your greatest moments have yet to come. Living a purposeful life is a commitment to personal development and positive change. The world-class traits discussed in this book, once developed, put your future in your hands.

If even one chapter resonated strongly enough with you to provoke a positive shift in your life, to me it means this book has served its purpose. But that decision to consciously improve your life will be because of you, not me. Only you can change you. Remember, positive change must first come from within. You could read a million pages in a million books, but the content won't matter unless you decide it's going to matter. While there are words to live by, only actions ignite true change and growth. Let your actions do the talking.

Know that personal development is a bumpy ride; be ready for the ups and downs. Making positive changes to your existing habits will not always seem positive in the moment, but the rewards will be indisputable. Start small. Focus on one or two positive changes you can make and build upon them. If you continue this process over time, you will wow yourself and others.

Always pursue progress over perfection. Try to be your best self every day, but remember that life will happen and life is not perfect. Although I try to live by the advice in this book every day, I won't always succeed (and I wrote the book!). Embrace the moments that make you human. There will be days when you don't bring your A game, when you put forth minimal effort, make bad decisions, or feel like giving up. These experiences, once acknowledged, provide you with the chance to reflect and come back stronger. With a superstar's mind-set, you will work to create a life that you love. The moments of struggle you endure will make your moments of success even better.

You are the leader of your life—the fact that you made it to this page tells me that. You are going to succeed, and the world is going to succeed because you are in it. In the words of human rights activist and Nobel Prize winner Malala Yousafzai, "Let us make our future now. And let us make our dreams tomorrow's reality." I thank you for caring about yourself and your future. It should put a smile on your face. It puts a smile on my face, because I know the future is in good hands. You know what you need to do; the rest, my friend, is up to you. Make every day count. Live. Learn. Develop. Go inspire yourself and others to greatness. Be the superstar that exists within you.

Enjoy life. Be smart.

—*Ryan*

Reflection and Self-Awareness Opportunity

1) *Start small—Look back through the chapter titles. What two chapters stand out as areas where you would most like to develop your superstar mind-set?*

    1.

    2.

Once you have incorporated these changes into your life, repeat this exercise until you have the total package.

2) *Final question. Which statement best describes you?*

    a) *Totally awesome*
    b) *Capable of anything you put your mind to*
    c) *In charge of your life's direction*
    d) *All of the above*

Answer: D

Epilogue
Together Is Better

Education is of paramount importance. The goal of this book is to help teenagers become superstars in life by emphasizing the upside of valuing themselves, their relationships, their time, and their opportunities in school.

Although this book focuses on the learner, we all play a vital role in making school a place where students can be inspired to best serve themselves and others.

Teachers must care, challenge students with realistically high expectations, grow personally and professionally, and create environments where learning, at each student's highest level, is possible and fun.

Students must also care, accept challenges to meet or exceed expectations, grow personally and academically, and immerse themselves in their school environments, making learning, at their highest levels, possible and fun.

Parents must love, encourage, and support their children in all educational pursuits.

And communities must create a culture where all of this is valued, encouraged, and expected.

Education is freedom. And with freedom, everything is possible.

Most sincerely,

Ryan Keliher

For more information about Ryan Keliher and *The Superstar Curriculum*, visit ryankeliher.com

64165563R00078

Made in the USA
Charleston, SC
26 November 2016